Totally AMAZING
SEA CREATURES

 A GOLDEN BOOK • NEW YORK

Golden Books Publishing Company, Inc., New York, New York 10106

Splashdown...
...into a Watery World

Nearly three-quarters of our world is covered with ocean. Creatures of every shape and size live there—from plankton, too tiny to see, to blue whales, which are the biggest animals on Earth.

That's Weird

Until recently, no one really knew what lurked beneath the waves. Centuries ago, sailors thought that the ocean was full of giant sea monsters.

Exploring the Deep

Today, scientists travel across the ocean floor in submersibles. They explore sandy seabeds, spooky caves, and rocky crags packed full of amazing creatures. The submersibles carry cameras for studying the creatures in detail.

Which Way Home?

Most sea creatures stick to their own patch of the ocean, where the temperature of the water suits them. Blue whales are at home in icy waters, but green sea turtles feel the cold, so they prefer warm seas. Bright parrot fish swim in shallow water near coral reefs and angler fish stick to deep, dark trenches.

What are you staring at?

2

Believe it or Not

A frogfish has joints on its fins. It can bend its fins just like you bend your elbows.

Come in—the water's great!

Frogfish scramble over hard coral, looking for smaller fish to snap up.

On the Move

Sea creatures move around in all sorts of strange ways. Some cut through the water with their sharp fins or bendy flippers. Others travel by squirting out water behind them. A few drifters just go where the ocean carries them.

Swimming Champion

You wouldn't stand a chance in a race with a sailfish. This torpedo-shaped record breaker is the ocean's fastest swimmer. It sails along at up to 67 miles (108 km) per hour, faster than a cheetah runs on land.

▲ A sea turtle is a powerful rowing machine that pulls its body through the water with oar-shaped flippers.

On the Wing

A manta ray flies through the ocean like a mysterious, underwater bird. This gentle giant flaps its wing-like fins up and down to move. The fins measure up to 26 feet (8 m) across, which is as wide as a two-seater airplane.

Little Squirts

To swim, a scallop quickly opens and closes its hinged shell, just like a pair of clicking castanets. Jets of water shoot out from the shell's two halves and push the creature through the ocean.

Under the Microscope

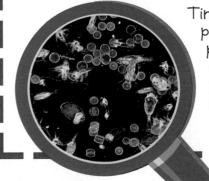

Tiny plankton are pushed along by powerful ocean currents. They provide food for many creatures.

Hiking Holiday

How would you like a long-distance hiking vacation? Once a year, lobsters make long journeys across the ocean floor. Eels travel great distances every year, too.

Are we there yet?

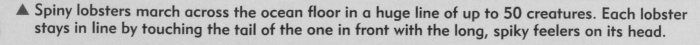

▲ Spiny lobsters march across the ocean floor in a huge line of up to 50 creatures. Each lobster stays in line by touching the tail of the one in front with the long, spiky feelers on its head.

Lobster Trek

Every autumn, off the coast of Florida, spiny lobsters head for deep waters to escape the violent fall storms that batter their home every year. The determined trekkers file across open plains where there are no hiding places. If an attacker strikes, the lobsters quickly make a circle and wave their snapping pincers to scare the enemy away.

I'm sure we were supposed to turn left back there.

Strange but True

Spiny lobsters walk for up to a week, traveling both day and night.

Sea Sounds

Sea creatures send love messages, chat to their babies, and even fire off warning signals. The ocean is rarely a quiet place!

Believe it or Not

A blue whale can shout 500 times louder than you can.

Shrimp with a Snap

Everyone knows when a pistol shrimp's in town. This creature fires off loud cracking sounds to scare its enemies. It snaps its claw together, making a sound like a gun shot, and its enemies run.

▲ Dolphins make more than 30 different sounds, including furious clicks and whistles. They are the ocean's champion gossips!

WHISTLES AND CLICKS

A male toadfish sings the perfect love song by vibrating a small sac inside his body. A female toadfish finds the noise irresistible. She swims towards him, he grabs her in his mouth and they head off to mate.

Mom?

A female dugong constantly shouts at her baby. As they swim through fields of murky seagrass along the coast, the baby hears the sound loud and clear, and knows its mother is within reach.

A Whale of a Time

The prize for the ocean's biggest animal goes to the mighty whale. Baleen whales are gentle giants that filter tiny animals into their mouths through bony plates called baleen. Whales with teeth are fierce hunters that snap up fish and squid.

That's Weird

A humpback whale is the opera singer of the deep. But listen too long and you're sure to get bored—the whale sings the same 30-minute song over and over again.

Deep-sea Battles

It's not a clever idea to get into a fight with a sperm whale. This animal is the largest toothed whale in the ocean. Sperm whales wrestle with giant squid underwater, and although it's not always an easy battle, the whale usually wins.

There She Blows!

Just like you, a whale breathes air. It swims to the surface of the ocean and blows out a towering, misty spray through blowholes on the top of its head. Then it takes a few deep breaths and down it goes again. This is one creature that is never left gasping for breath.

Strange but True
Every now and then, whales leap out of the water. This is called breaching. No one has any idea why they do this.

A humpback whale has incredibly long flippers, which it holds out for balance when it leaps. Its giant flippers also provide perfect shelter for its young calves.

Underwater **Garden**

Beautiful gardens, called coral reefs, stretch across parts of the ocean floor. Dazzling, tiny fish dart through this fantastical world.

EXPLORING A REEF

▲ There are hundreds of different kinds of coral, from swaying fans and branches to brain-shaped coral!

Under the Microscope

These look like plants but really they are tiny sea animals called coral polyps.

Sworn Enemies

The crown-of-thorns starfish is the coral reef's number one enemy. A hungry pack of these starfish can chomp through so much coral that they turn the reef into a dead zone.

BURP!!

Family Matters

Most sea creatures lay their eggs and swim off into the sunset. But a few proud parents stick around until their eggs hatch.

HOW A FLATFISH CHANGES FACES

When it's born, a baby flatfish looks like any other young fish, with an eye on each side of its head.

Hey, I look just like you!

As the flatfish grows older, its body becomes flatter. It lives on the seabed with one eye stuck in the sand.

Mmm, everything's blurred now.

This eye travels round to join the other one. It can see better now, with both eyes on the same side of its head!

That's better.

You look weird!

Nanny Patrol

After laying her eggs, a female lumpsucker leaves a male in charge. He keeps the eggs cool by fanning them frantically with his fin until they hatch. He also shoos away hungry crabs.

That's Weird

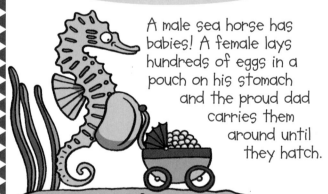

A male sea horse has babies! A female lays hundreds of eggs in a pouch on his stomach and the proud dad carries them around until they hatch.

Operation Turtle

A baby sea turtle's first steps are a dangerous adventure. The turtle hatches in the dark of night and makes a mad dash across the sand to the safety of the sea. On the way, pecking birds and hungry crabs may gobble it up.

Beastly Babes

Sand tiger sharks are fearsome fish, even before they are born. Unlike most sea creatures, they do not hatch from eggs but grow inside their mother's body. As they grow, the bigger babies eat their smaller brothers and sisters. This ferocious family feast continues until there are only two extremely strong tiger sharks left.

Strange but True

Female turtles swim back to the sandy beaches where they were born to lay their eggs.

Hatching from an egg can be hard work. Turtle eggs are buried deep beneath the sand and the babies have to dig their way to the surface using their flippers.

Marine Meals...

...and Fishy Desserts

Sea creatures dine out in different ways. Some are roaming hunters with sneaky methods of catching prey. Others just wait for a tasty treat to turn up.

Floating Feast

Sea squirts have their food delivered. These swaying sea animals are rooted to the spot and wait for plankton to drift by. As sea squirts suck in water through a hole in their bodies, yummy plankton drift in too.

Bloodsucker

A hagfish is like a vampire. It attaches its sucker-like mouth to another fish. Then it grinds away at its victim' flesh with its horny teeth and feasts on its blood.

Tell Me Why

A SEA OTTER NEEDS A KITCHEN TOOL

Believe it or Not

Some octopuses stun their prey with a shot of poison before eating it.

▲ This octopus is eating a dogfish. With the octopus's eight waggling arms grabbing it from all sides, the fish didn't have a chance.

A sea otter carries a stone under its arm, which it uses like a nutcracker. First, the otter dives down to the ocean floor to find its meal. It usually chooses its favorite food—sea urchins.

Burnt to a Crisp

Small fish often come to a sizzling end when they wander too close to a torpedo ray. This spine-tingling creature gives its prey a sharp electric shock before munching it up.

Next, the otter swims up to the surface of the water. It lies on its back and smashes the sea urchins against the stone. Now the otter can reach the juicy meat inside.

17

Shark Attack!

One of the scariest creatures in the ocean is the great white shark. This monster of the deep has an excellent sense of smell. It can sniff out the faintest scent of blood. It also has razor-sharp teeth that tear off chunks of flesh.

That's Weird

A hammerhead is a very strange-looking shark. Its huge head is shaped like the end of a hammer, with eyes at either end for perfect all-round vision.

Man-eating Mistakes

Sharks rarely go after people and most kinds are shy. If they do attack, it's probably because they've made a mistake. Scientists think that some great white sharks have attacked surfers because they thought they were seals.

Believe it or Not

In its lifetime, a great white shark grows hundreds of jagged teeth, each one as long as your finger.

HA HA! Why is it easy to fool a shark? Because it'll swallow anything. HEE HEE!

I'd move out of the way, if I were you.

▲ A great white shark cruises silently through the water. It beats its huge tail from side to side to swim.

Escape Tactics

Nearly every sea creature has enemies that can't wait to gobble it up. Surprise tactics are often the best method of escape.

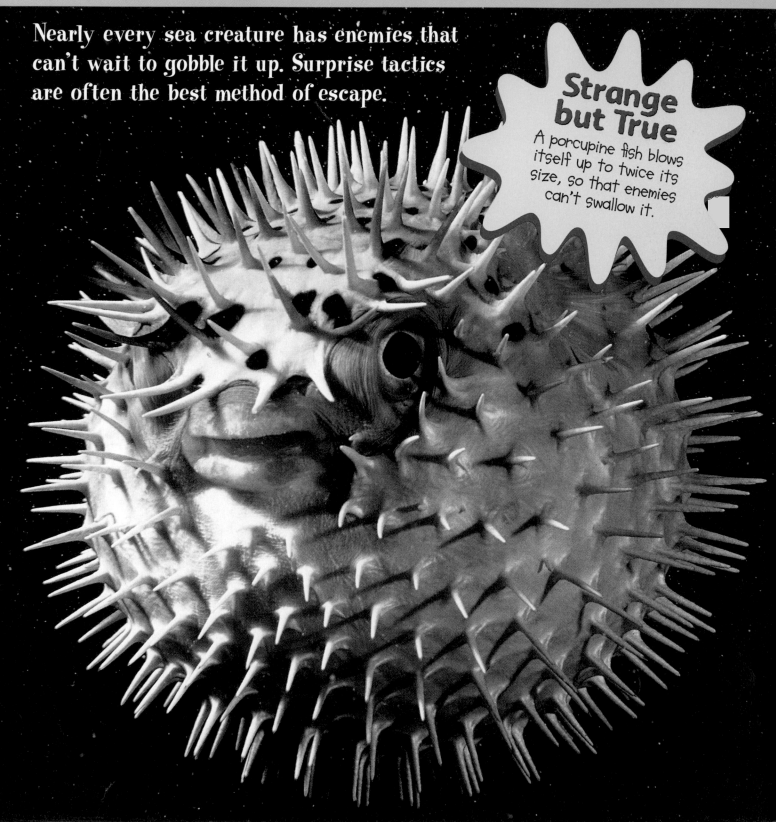

Strange but True
A porcupine fish blows itself up to twice its size, so that enemies can't swallow it.

▲ This porcupine fish has gulped in mouthfuls of water to make itself look like a spiky monster.

Safety in Shoals

Swimming together in roving packs, called shoals, is one way to stay safe. Scientists think that small fish may swim in huge shoals to make themselves look like one enormous fish. If the fish are attacked, they scatter in all directions, confusing their enemy.

That's Weird

Is it a bird? Is it a plane? No, it's a flying fish! When a flying fish is chased, it leaps out of the water and spreads out its fins to glide to safety.

Hey, get back here!

Ink-credible!

An octopus is like an ink pen. When it's attacked, it squirts out a huge cloud of black ink. The attacker can't see a thing and the octopus makes a quick getaway.

Tell Me How

CRABS LOSE THEIR LEGS BUT NOT THEIR HEADS

How did it get away?

Crabs escape from hungry mouths by leaving bits of their bodies behind. When a crab is caught by its leg, the leg snaps off. It even has special weak points to help it break off more easily.

The crab quickly hobbles away. After a few months, the missing leg grows back, but it may be much smaller than the other ones. Still, it's a lucky escape!

21

The Great Cover Up

Sea creatures are masters of disguise. In the blink of an eye, they dress up or change color to blend in with their surroundings. This stops them from being eaten by hungry predators.

Believe it or Not

A butterfly fish wears false eyes on its tail to confuse its enemies.

All Change

Flatfish, such as flounder and turbot, are real quick-change artists. They can turn from one color to another in minutes to hide themselves. If you put a flatfish on a chessboard, it will even become checkered!

CRABBY CLOTHING

When a spider crab arrives at a beach, it gathers a pile of seaweed and designs a new outfit.

I hate to stand out from the crowd.

The crab arranges the seaweed on its shell. Tiny spines on the crab's body hold it in place. Now it's almost invisible.

Where did it go?

When the crab moves on, it sheds its old clothes for new ones that are more suited to its surroundings.

A sponge suit would be nice.

▼ A stonefish is much more dangerous than it looks. Step on it and you'll be injected with a nasty poison!

Sinister Stone

You need to be a hot-shot detective to discover a stonefish. This warty creature sits on the ocean floor, looking like a seaweed-covered rock that's been there for thousands of years. But there is a point to the fish's dull days. When small fish swim by, the stonefish opens its mouth and gobbles them up.

That's Weird

A lionfish is one of the ocean's biggest show-offs. Its dazzling stripes warn other fish that its spines are full of deadly poison!

I'm lethal.

23

Sticking Together..

...Perfect Pals

Many sea creatures help each other out. These partnerships are often the best way for creatures to survive in this watery world

▲ When a hermit crab moves into a new shell, it takes its partner, the sea anemone, with it. It pulls the anemone off the old shell and gets it to attach itself to the new one.

Perfect Protection

A sea anemone and a hermit crab are seasoned travelers. The anemone hitches a ride with the crab and protects it with its poisonous tentacles. In return, the anemone gets a ride across the ocean floor and stops for lunch on the way.

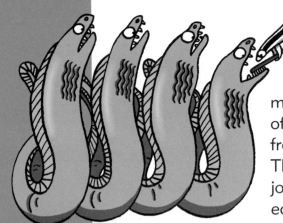

Wash and Scrub

A cleaner wrasse offers a cleaning service for moray eels. The wrasse picks off dead skin and leftover food from between the eel's teeth. The wrasse is so good at its job that often it has several eager eels waiting in line.

That's Weird

You won't find happier roommates than a blind shrimp and a goby fish. The shrimp cleans house while the goby watches out for intruders.

Air Ambulance

Dolphins live in families that are trained in first-aid. When a dolphin family member becomes ill, relatives lift it gently to the surface of the water so that it can breathe. The caring cousins also fight off unwelcome enemies.

Taking a nap can be a dangerous business in the ocean. Sea creatures have found ingenious ways to stay safe while they have a quick and well-earned snooze.

Sweet Dreams

Rocky Retreat

Despite its huge size, a giant octopus can wedge itself into a tiny crack. The hole is so small that nothing else can climb in.

Strange but True

Fish have no eyelids. They sleep with their eyes open.

Brain Power

It's not easy to fool a dolphin, even when it's asleep. When a dolphin takes a nap, only half of its brain shuts down. The other half works overtime, just in case danger strikes.

▲ An octopus prefers the night-shift. During the day, it snoozes but at night it crawls across the ocean floor on the hunt for food.

That's Weird

A parrot fish sleeps in a bubble. When it's about to rest, a jelly-like substance oozes out of its body and blows up into a cozy cocoon.

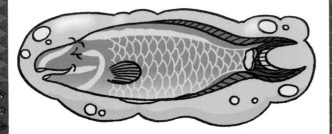

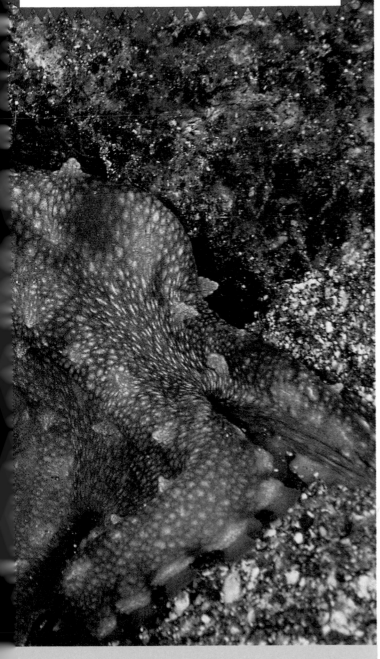

Making the Bed

Sea otters always remember to make their beds. When they bunker down for the evening, these furry little creatures wrap themselves in a cozy blanket of giant kelp, which is a type of seaweed. The kelp is rooted to the ocean floor and stops the otters from drifting in the current.

Hired Help

A clownfish has a sea anemone as its personal bodyguard. It rests between the anemone's poisonous, waving tentacles, knowing that enemies will suffer a sharp sting if they come too close!

Ouch! That hurts.

Deeply Creepy!

Who Switched off the Lights?

Thousands of feet below the ocean's surface, it is freezing cold and pitch black. Many weird-looking creatures have adapted to living in these inky depths.

Balancing Act

A tripod fish looks a bit like a three-legged stool. It lives on the bottom of the ocean, propping itself up on its extra-long tail and fins to stop itself from sinking into the mud. Here it waits hoping for a tasty snack to drift by.

I'm not that scary when you get to know me.

Shrimp. My favorite!

▲ A scary-looking viper fish hunts for food with its huge mouth wide open. In the dark, small fish can't see its mouth. They swim straight inside and come to a bone-crunching end.

Back from the Dead

One day, in 1938, a group of fishermen had a real shock. They caught an odd-looking fish that they had never seen before. Scientists told them later that it was a coelacanth, a deep-sea fish which was thought to have died out over 70 million years ago!

I can't see a thing.

At least we're warm.

Smoking Chimney

Can you imagine living next door to a chimney that belches out black smoke day and night? Huge groups of giant tubeworms grow on rocky stacks on the ocean floor which spurt out hot water and gases. The tubeworms never eat. Instead, bacteria inside their bodies make food for them.

SOME DEEP-SEA FISH HAVE BRIGHT IDEAS

An angler fish catches its food with a glowing fishing rod dangling from its head. The fish waggles the rod and its prey swims towards it, fascinated by the light.

A flashlight fish has pouches under its eyes that are like a pair of blinking headlights. The fish quickly switches its headlights on and off to find a mate in the dark.

All Star Aquarium

The oceans are packed with superstars. Some are big, others are small, and a few are rare or deadly. But they are all record-breakers.

Big Blue

The blue whale is the biggest star of the ocean. This heavyweight is the largest animal ever to have lived in water or on land. It weighs more than 25 elephants.

Killer on the Loose

Watch out for the box jellyfish, the most poisonous sea creature. Its body is small, but its tentacles grow up to 9 feet (3 m) long. If anything brushes past them, they shoot out tiny poison darts that can kill a human in minutes.

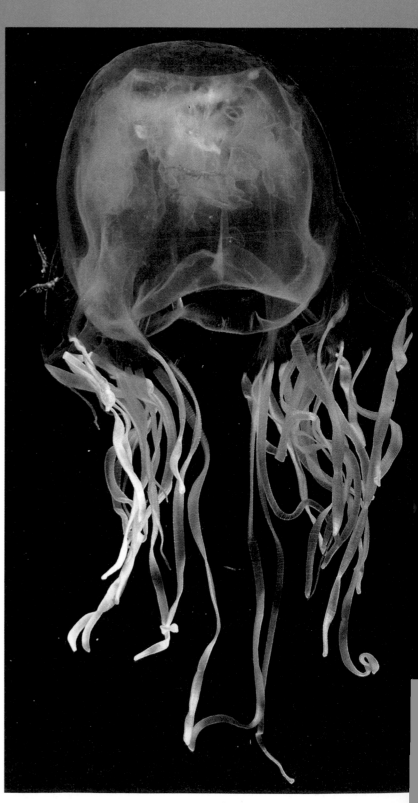

Smile Please

The whale shark is a double winner. It's the biggest fish, and has the largest mouth of any fish. It swims along with its mouth open in a grin wide enough to swallow a man. Luckily, it eats only plankton and a few other tiny fish.

Prize for Size

The tiny pea crab wins the trophy for the smallest crab. This pea-sized creature lives squeezed inside the shell of a live oyster. It munches the oyster's food, safe from enemies.

The spider crab of Japan claims the largest crab trophy. This giant can grow as big as 12 feet (3.7 m) across from the tip of one outstretched claw to the other. Its legs are long enough to give a hippo a hug!

Old Timer

The Golden Oldie medal goes to an eel that was born in the sea, then caught in a river, and kept in an aquarium. This ancient grandma lived to the ripe old age of 88!

Deep-sea Diver

In a diving competition, a sperm whale leaves a human way behind. The whale can hold its breath for 90 minutes and dive at least 20 times deeper than any human.

Index and Glossary

Illustrations: Andrew Peters
Consultant: Dr Frances Dipper
Author: Iqbal Hussain
Photographs: p1: The Stock Market; p3: Planet Earth pictures; p4/5: The Stock Market; p5 top & bottom right: Planet Earth Pictures; p6/7: Oxford Scientific Films; p8/9: Robert Harding Picture Library; p11: Tony Stone Images; p12/13: Planet Earth Pictures; p15: Powerstock; p16 left: Planet Earth Pictures; p16/17: Oxford Scientific Films; p18/19: Ardea London Ltd; p20: Tony Stone Images; p21: Planet Earth Pictures; p23: Planet Earth Pictures; p24/25: Planet Earth Pictures; p26/27: The Stock Market; p27: BBC Natural History Unit Picture Library; p28: Planet Earth Pictures; p29: Planet Earth Pictures; p30: Planet Earth Pictures; p31: Tony Stone Images.